ANCIENT GREECE AND THE OLYMPICS

Children's Ancient History

BABY PROFESSOR

EDUCATION KIDS

Speedy Publishing LLC

40 E. Main St. #1156

Newark, DE 19711

www.speedypublishing.com

Copyright 2017

In this book, we're going to talk about the first Olympic Games. So, let's get right to it!

MOUNT OLYMPUS

THE ANCIENT GREEK OLYMPICS

The Olympic Games that we know of today were written about in 776 BC, around 3,000 years ago, but they were started centuries earlier. They began as part of a religious ceremony to honor the king of all the Greek gods and goddesses, who was called Zeus. The Greeks believed that Zeus held court on the peak of Mount Olympus, which was the country's tallest mountain.

Even though the name of the games sounds like Mount Olympus, the games were not held there. Instead, they were held in the beautiful city of Olympia on the southwest coast of the country. The region was a sanctuary that was rich with sacred olive trees.

TEMPLE OF ZEUS

◊ver time, the games became incredibly popular and well attended. They were held consistently every four years from the first game in 776 BC to the last game in 393 AD—over one thousand years!

THE PANHELLENIC GAMES

There were four sports festivals that were held on a regular basis during Ancient Greek times. They were called the panhellenic games. The games were:

The Olympic Games, which were the most important of all four games and held in honor of Zeus every four years in Olympia and Elis

ANCIENT OLYMPIA

POSEIDON

The Pythian Games, which were held every four years on a different cycle than the Olympics in honor of the sun god Apollo and near the location of Delphi

The Nemean Games, which were also in honor of Zeus and were celebrated every two years near Nemea

The Isthmian Games, which were held every two years in honor of the sea god Poseidon near the city of Corinth

These games were so important to Greek culture that they used the four-year cycle that was called the Olympiad as a way to tell time. The Olympic Games

were celebrated in the first year of the four-year cycle. Then, the Nemean as well as the Isthmian Games were held in the second year of the cycle, both in different months.

GREECE, OLYMPIA

The Pythian Games took place in year three and then the Nemean and Isthmian were repeated again in year four before the cycle started all over again. The cycle was structured in this way so that athletes would have the opportunity to play in all the games if they wished.

Athletes came from all over the Greek civilization including the Greek colonies, which at that time included areas of Asia Minor and Spain.

WHO COMPETED IN THE ANCIENT OLYMPICS?

Slaves were not allowed to compete in the events. Free men who were youthful and athletic were encouraged to participate. Historians are not certain if there was a specific age requirement, but the endurance that was needed meant that older men probably didn't participate.

ZEUS

One of the other requirements was that the participants had to be fluent in Greek. Women were not allowed to participate as a rule, but records exist that show a woman who won an event, possibly as the owner of a chariot that was raced. All participants had to swear in honor of Zeus that they had been in training to prepare for the event for at least ten months.

It wasn't inexpensive to participate in the games. Participants probably had to be fairly well off to pay for all the transportation and lodging as well as the training needed to participate in the events.

KOTINOS

The winners were rewarded with olive branches from an olive tree that the Greeks considered sacred called the kotinos. The Olympic athletes and other athletes from the Panhellenic Games became famous and sometimes wealthy from these competitions. In their hometowns, they were admired and favored by the citizens they represented, just like our Olympic athletes are today.

WHAT TYPES OF GAMES WERE HELD IN THE ANCIENT OLYMPICS?

The first Olympic Games were foot races that were relatively short. They were designed to help men stay in peak shape for battle. The path was 700 feet in length and it was straight, but it was so wide that 20 men could compete against each other lined up side to side. This event was called the stadion after the building that was built to house the race.

STADIUM IN OLYMPIA

Men ran these foot races without any clothes on. The games were played in late July or early August. As the events went on throughout the years, more types

of athletic competitions were added. Unlike today's modern Olympics there were no team competitions.

There were also no Olympic medals. Only one winner was crowned with sacred leaves from the special olive tree located at the temple to Zeus in Olympia. Winners often had statues constructed in their honor.

TEMPLE OF ZEUS

CHARIOT RACING

In addition to the stadion race and foot races of various lengths, the events that were added to the Ancient Olympics were:

Chariot Racing—These races with horse-drawn chariots took place in the Hippodrome, which was a wide, open space.

Wrestling—This event was considered to be a military activity without weaponry. It ended when one opponent admitted defeat.

Boxing—Boxers had special straps wrapped on their hands to make their wrists stronger and their fingers more steady.

Pankration—This was a very early form of martial art that mixed wrestling and boxing and was one of the most difficult sports to master.

Pentathlon—Which was made up of five different competitions of the long jump, the discus and javelin throws, the stadion, and wrestling

BOXING

WRESTLING

Even though some of these events are named the same as events we have today, the rules were different and the games were much more dangerous. Boxing and wrestling were not regulated as much as they are today.

Generally in boxing, even if your opponent was down on the ground you could continue to attack him. The match wasn't over until a fighter conceded or died. It wasn't a smart idea to eliminate your opponent because those that died in the match were awarded an automatic victory.

HERA

DID WOMEN ATTEND?

Married women were not given permission to either watch or participate in the events. There was a festival called Heraia in honor of Hera, Zeus's wife that married women were allowed to attend. In today's modern Olympic Games women can be attendees as well as participants.

HOW LONG WERE THE GAMES HELD?

The games had been held over one thousand years until they were banned by Theodosius, the Roman emperor, in 393 AD. The Greek civilization had been overtaken by the new power in the Mediterranean—the Romans.

THEODOSIUS

PARTHENON

The Roman Empire was quickly converting to Christianity and the emperor wanted to outlaw worship of the pagan gods. The games were associated with the Ancient gods and goddesses so he shut them down. The buildings were eventually destroyed and the city as it stood in antiquity was devastated by floods and earthquakes.

A TRUCE SO THE GAMES COULD BEGIN

At the height of the popularity of the Ancient Olympics more than 40,000 people were attendees. The Olympics even became more important than the never-ending battles between the city-states. The Ancient Greeks adopted a special truce that occurred a month before the games began.

OLYMPIC STADIUM ENTRANCE

OLYMPIC STADIUM, ATHENS

During this truce, men could prepare for the events and attendees could travel to get to the location without fear. They could even pass through enemy territory without being attacked. Vendors came to sell their food and other souvenirs of the games.

The games generally took place over five days with the first and last day designed to honor the gods, sometimes with animal sacrifices. To honor Zeus, one hundred oxen were sacrificed.

GREECE OLYMPIC RUINS

PIERRE DE COUBERTIN

THE MODERN OLYMPICS

The Ancient Olympics ended in 393 AD and it was 1,503 years before they were started again by Pierre de Coubertin. Pierre was a French historian and educator who loved sporting events. He thought that the countries that played in competitions together would get to know each other's cultures better, which would promote peaceful relations.

Pierre designed the beautiful five-color Olympic logo. The rings represent the continents—North and South America, Australia and Europe as well as Africa and Asia.

DEM MITONFHEREP DEP

The idea of the Olympic torch was first launched at the games held in Amsterdam in 1928. Torch relays happened in Ancient times but the tradition of the torch is different today. A torch is lit at the beginning of the event. The flame is carried from the city of Olympia and is carefully passed from torch to torch until the final location is reached. The Olympics are held all over the world and the location changes each time they are held.

Today, the Olympic Games are the largest and most well attended sports event worldwide. There are games played in both winter and summer and the games have been extended to incorporate over 30 different sports. People from all different countries compete for the coveted medals made of bronze, silver, and gold.

ANCIENT OLYMPIC EVENT

Awesome! Now you know more about the Olympic Games that were played during the Ancient Greek civilization. You can find more Ancient History books from Baby Professor by searching the website of your favorite book retailer.

Visit

BABY PROFESSOR
EDUCATION KIDS

www.BabyProfessorBooks.com

to download Free Baby Professor eBooks and view
our catalog of new and exciting Children's Books

CPSIA information can be obtained
at www.ICGtesting.com
Printed in the USA
BVHW091641160622
639855BV00007B/441

9 781541 911215